This journal belongs to:

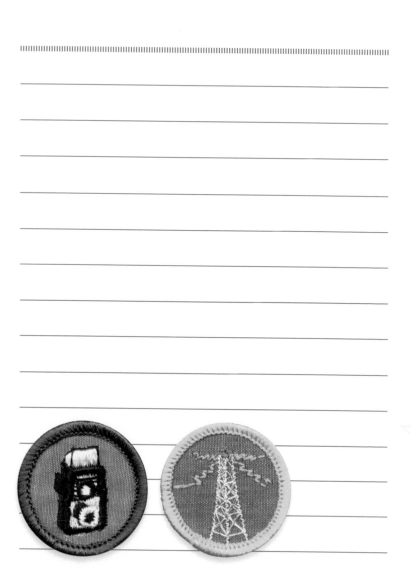

_____

_____

_____

_____

_____

_____

_____

_____

_____

_____

_____

_____

_____

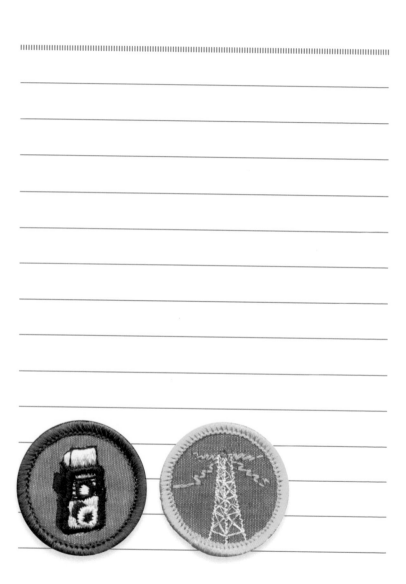

_____

_____

_____

_____

_____

_____

_____

_____

_____

_____

_____

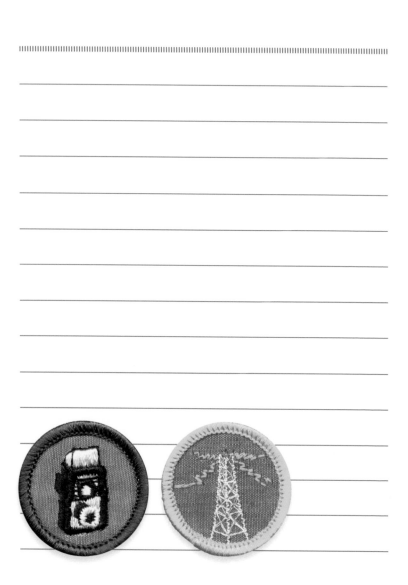

_____

_____

_____

_____

_____

_____

_____

_____

_____

_____

_____

_____

1956 GIRL SCOUT
SENIOR ROUNDUP
N
W E
S

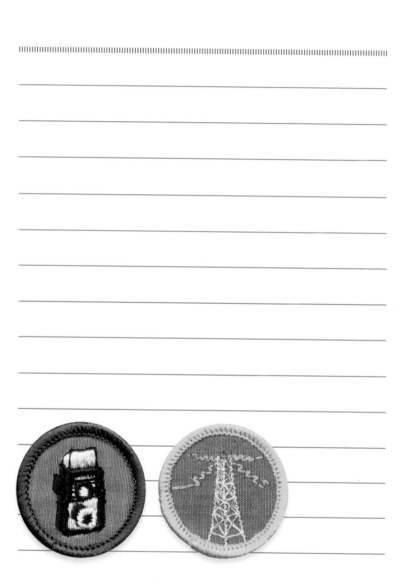

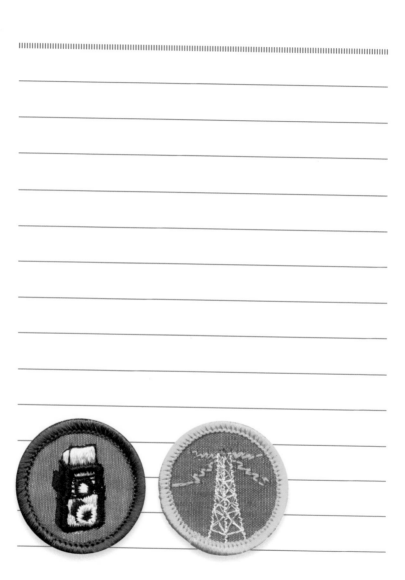

_____

_____

_____

_____

_____

_____

_____

_____

_____

_____

_____

_____

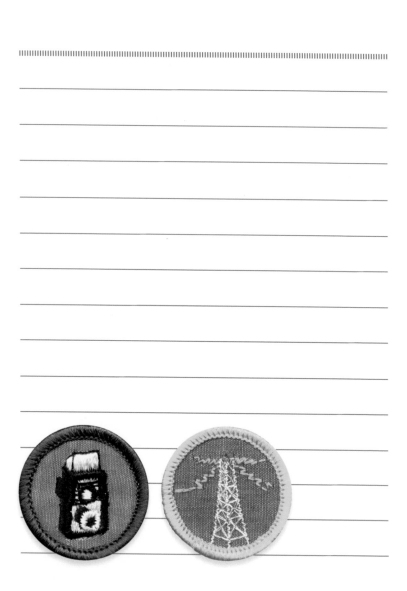

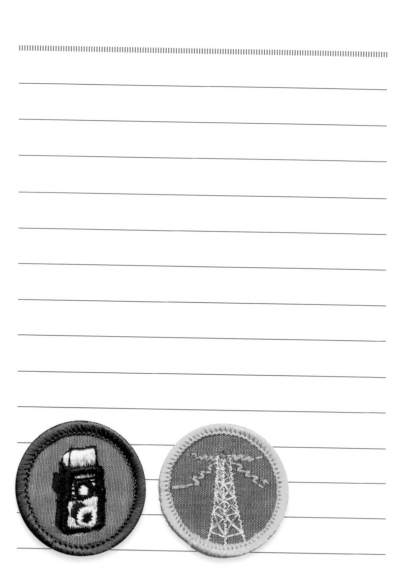

_____

_____

_____

_____

_____

_____

_____

_____

_____

_____

_____

_____

1956 GIRL SCOUT SENIOR ROUNDUP

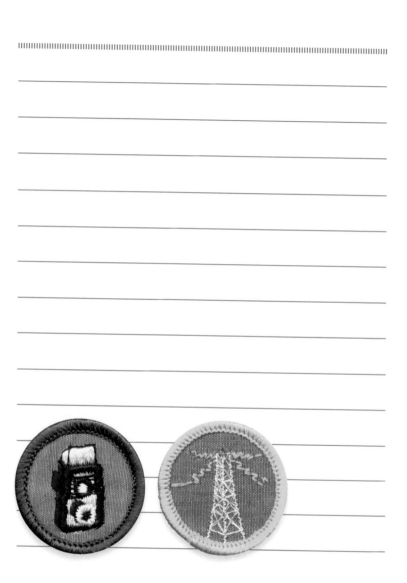

_____

_____

_____

_____

_____

_____

_____

_____

_____

_____

_____

_____

1956 GIRL SCOUT
SENIOR ROUNDUP
N W E S

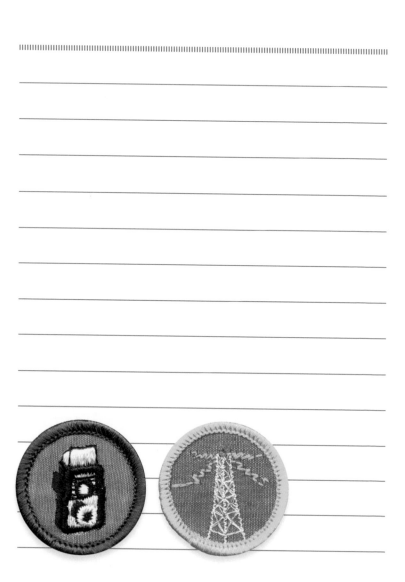

_____

_____

_____

_____

_____

_____

_____

_____

_____

_____

_____

_____

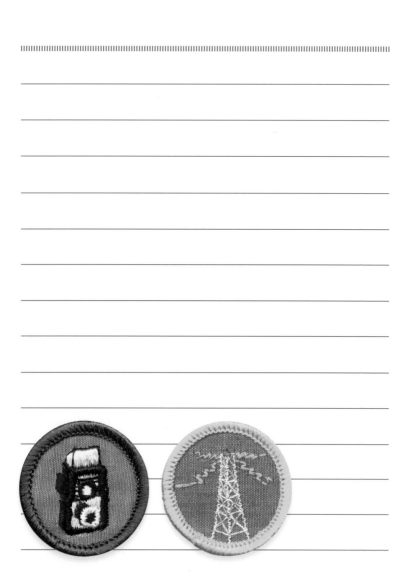

_____

_____

_____

_____

_____

_____

_____

_____

_____

_____

_____

_____

_____

1956 GIRL SCOUT
SENIOR ROUNDUP
N W E S

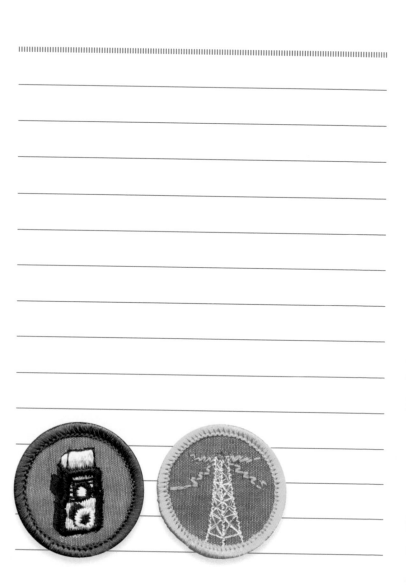

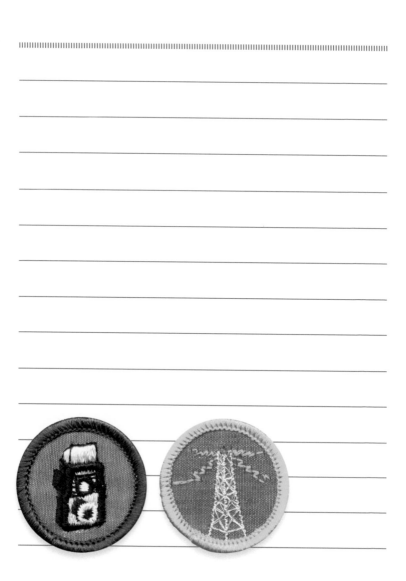

_____

_____

_____

_____

_____

_____

_____

_____

_____

_____

_____

_____

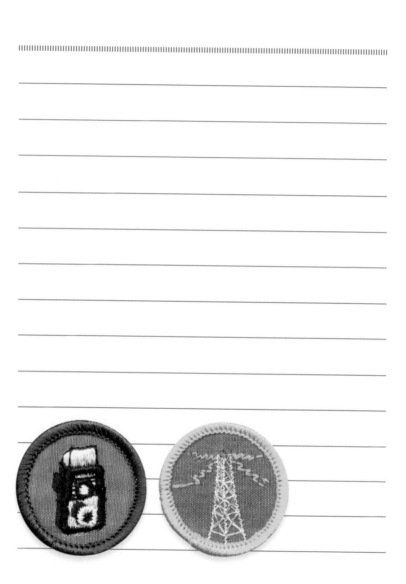

_____

_____

_____

_____

_____

_____

_____

_____

_____

_____

_____

_____

_____

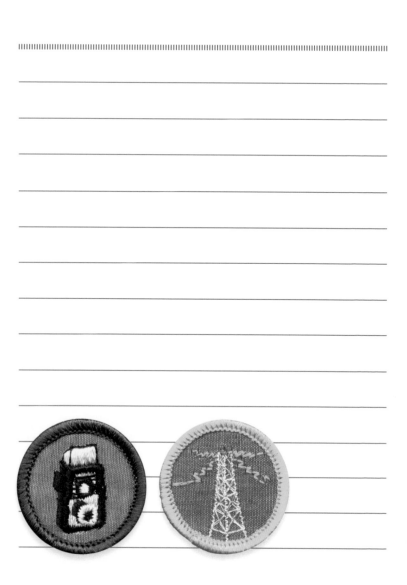

_____

_____

_____

_____

_____

_____

_____

_____

_____

_____

_____

_____

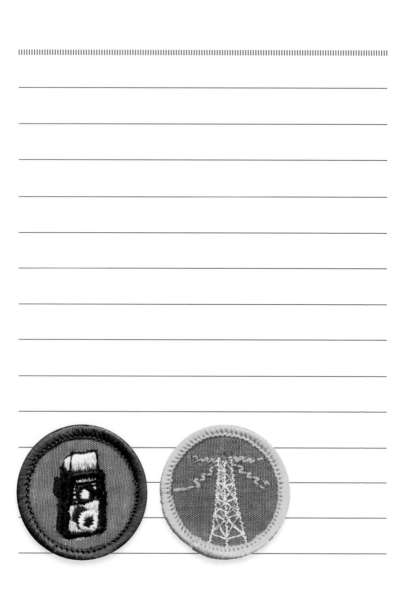

_____

_____

_____

_____

_____

_____

_____

_____

_____

_____

_____

_____

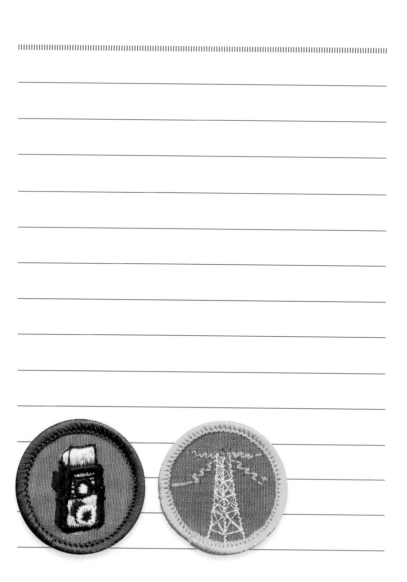

_____

_____

_____

_____

_____

_____

_____

_____

_____

_____

_____

_____

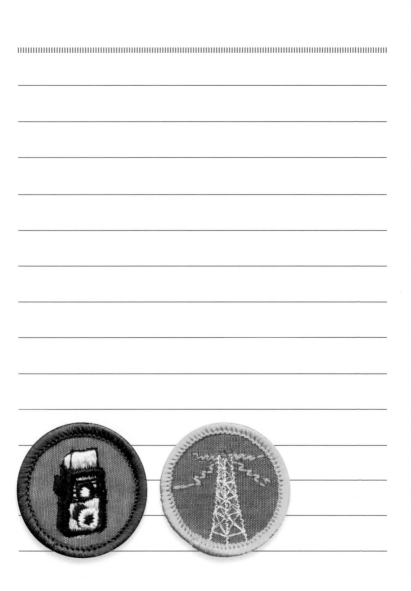

1956 GIRL SCOUT SENIOR ROUNDUP

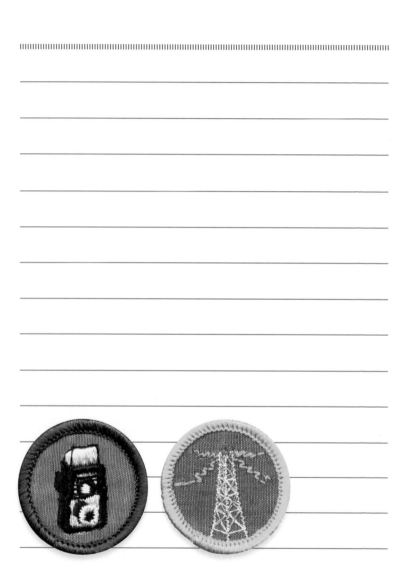

_____

_____

_____

_____

_____

_____

_____

_____

_____

_____

_____

1956 GIRL SCOUT
SENIOR ROUNDUP
N
W E
S

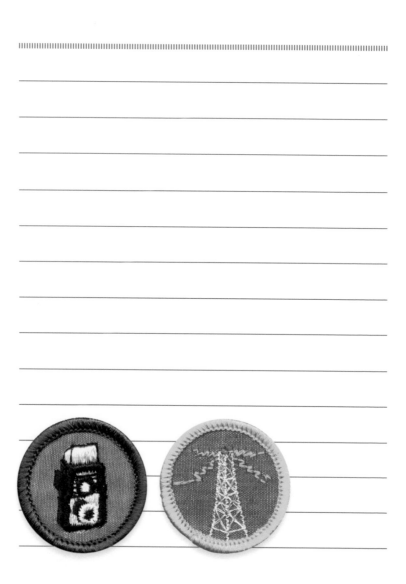

_____

_____

_____

_____

_____

_____

_____

_____

_____

_____

_____

_____

1956 GIRL SCOUT SENIOR ROUNDUP

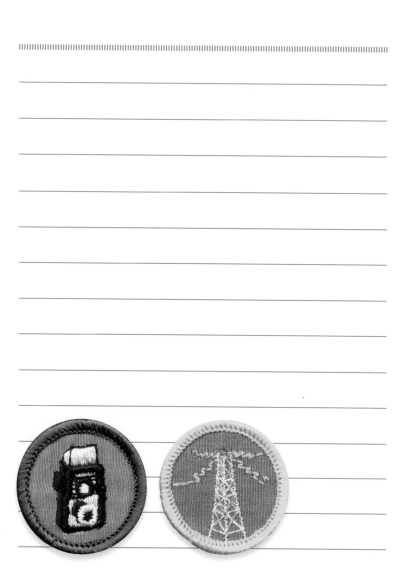

_____

_____

_____

_____

_____

_____

_____

_____

_____

_____

_____

_____

1956 GIRL SCOUT SENIOR ROUNDUP

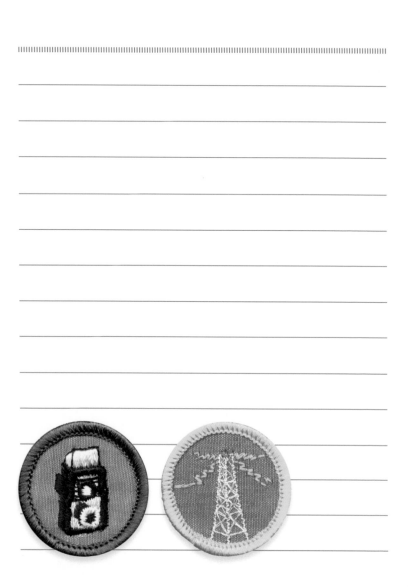

_____

_____

_____

_____

_____

_____

_____

_____

_____

_____

_____

_____

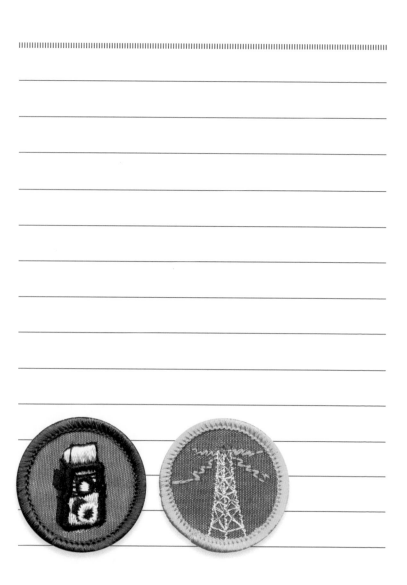

_____

_____

_____

_____

_____

_____

_____

_____

_____

_____

_____

_____

1956 GIRL SCOUT SENIOR ROUNDUP

_____

_____

_____

_____

_____

_____

_____

_____

_____

_____

_____

_____